Blue Sky
THOUGHTS

Positive Insights for Everyday Life

Gary Muller

BALBOA PRESS

A DIVISION OF HAY HOUSE

Author Photo by Nyssa Bilsborough

Balboa Press books may be ordered through booksellers or by contacting:

Balboa Press
A Division of Hay House
1663 Liberty Drive
Bloomington, IN 47403
www.balboapress.com.au
1 (877) 407-4847

Because of the dynamic nature of the Internet, any web addresses or links contained in this book may have changed since publication and may no longer be valid. The views expressed in this work are solely those of the author and do not necessarily reflect the views of the publisher, and the publisher hereby disclaims any responsibility for them.

The author of this book does not dispense medical advice or prescribe the use of any technique as a form of treatment for physical, emotional, or medical problems without the advice of a physician, either directly or indirectly. The intent of the author is only to offer information of a general nature to help you in your quest for emotional and spiritual well-being. In the event you use any of the information in this book for yourself, which is your constitutional right, the author and the publisher assume no responsibility for your actions.

Any people depicted in stock imagery provided by Thinkstock are models, and such images are being used for illustrative purposes only. Certain stock imagery © Thinkstock.

Print information available on the last page.

ISBN: 978-1-5043-0405-4 (sc)
ISBN: 978-1-5043-0406-1 (e)

Balboa Press rev. date: 08/25/2016

DEDICATION

To my beautiful wife, Gail Muller, whose love, support, and encouragement have made all of my dreams become reality.

INTRODUCTION

As a younger man, I was very naïve about life and knew nothing about who I was. Blissfully ignorant would be a great way to describe me. I was an open book and trusted people too easily, expecting that people always had the right intentions. Over the years, I had to learn many difficult lessons, some time and time again. Without actually knowing it, I had virtually no self-esteem or self-worth, and this created problems for me in every area of my life. I unknowingly allowed the judgements, criticisms, and opinions of others to form my own self-image and self-worth. Life was controlling me instead of me controlling life. The never-ending illusions of bad luck, wrong time, wrong person, and victim mentality seemed to haunt me. I actually believed that my place in the world could never change. It was a horrible feeling.

When I reached forty years of age, I found myself at the crossroads. Finally gaining my qualifications as a commercial pilot, after a lot of expense and years of training, the reality that I was not gaining employment in this area and at my age was very difficult to accept. I had left my job of fifteen years to pursue this dream, and it had not worked out. Another failed relationship, unemployment, and being short of money were taking a toll on my already low self-esteem. This was to be a very defining moment in my life. I was forced to confront some of the issues that had been limiting me for decades. It was to lead me to find my passion, my purpose, and my true meaning. The journey of self-discovery, awareness, and unconditional love arrived out of a very difficult time in my life.

My quest for answers was growing stronger. Before I knew it, they were arriving in unexpected ways. Meeting the right people, being in the right place, and asking the right questions led me further in the right direction. The decision to start healing myself and the past became a mission that demanded priority. There was a lot of soul-searching, forgiveness, and responsibility to be taken in order to build a new foundation. Before I knew it, I was qualified in spiritual healing and reiki therapy. The journey was only beginning, and there would still be much work to be done, but I had finally begun.

After several years of searching and healing, I made the decision to devote my life to helping others to do the same. This began with me undertaking volunteer work in the counselling and community-support fields. At the age of forty-four, I went back to full-time study and attained my diploma of counselling. In 2012, I began my own mobile counselling practice in Adelaide, South Australia called Blue Sky Counselling Service, which will soon be changed to Blue Sky Horizons. I appear on a local Adelaide radio station as a guest counsellor every fortnight.

Blue Sky Thoughts began as a dream, a fantasy that seemed so unrealistic. Imagine having my words published and shared with the world. The desire to help raise people's awareness and teach them about what they can achieve has willed this book into reality. It is the culmination of my professional training, teaching from mentors, and fifty-two years of my own life experience. Each insight has been derived from lessons that I have had to learn, some more than once. The two greatest influences in helping me to create this book are my darling wife, Gail, whose unconditional love, support, and encouragement have made me believe in miracles, and the wonderful Dr. Wayne W. Dyer. We were honoured to meet Wayne last year in Melbourne. His teaching and love have inspired me to take my work to a new level.

We are all deserving, we are all worthy, we are all capable, we are all powerful, and when we finally believe it, we will finally see it. Wishing you much love and light on your personal journey.

Peaceful feelings are not things we have to buy, negotiate for, or strive to get. They are not foreign to us. Nor do they separate us from our true natures. Peaceful feelings are a natural aspect of who we are; they are an aspect of our souls. They are as natural as our physical bodies, but so many of us struggle to connect with them. The reason is the ego. We become immersed in our heads, and that will tell us we need to panic, be stressed, be anxious, be depressed, and be fearful. It tells us we can't be happy, safe, or content. This is an illusion; we can connect to peaceful feelings anytime we choose to. All we need to do is be willing to practice. All of life is dictated by our perspectives. I have seen how we can change our perspectives and, therefore, change our lives. When we stop struggling, we become peaceful and create positive change.

Sometimes things need to get to a breaking point before we see the light. This has happened to me more times than I care to remember. Part of us always knows what needs to happen, but we can become stubborn, fearful, and too proud. Or we may pretend that everything really is all right. The result is that things stay the same or even get worse. If we learn to feel with our hearts instead of being stuck in our heads, we receive the answers and guidance we need.

Many years ago I was told that nobody would cause me more harm than I would cause myself. And I believe it. We all get in our own way at times. However, don't forget that sometimes things need to get to a certain point before we can see the light. Learn to feel with your heart and then verify with your head, not the other way around.

Since I have been living in the moment, I have enjoyed each day for what it is—a gift. I am more aware of what is happening and what I need to do. There have been more love and abundance, and a feeling of contentment. It is nice to know that I can practice what I teach my clients with full confidence in knowing it works.

Living in the past serves no useful purpose. If we stay living in the past for long enough, it is very likely to lead to depression. Living in the future is also pointless because you have no power in the future. Those always living in the future, trying to work out everything before it happens, are likely to experience anxiety. You only have power right now, in the present. Make the most of your life by being present in each moment. Then you can create a better future for yourself.

Everyone, everything, and every part of us has a connection, whether we like it or not. Within ourselves, the mental, emotional, physical, and spiritual are all connected. This means what affects one aspect of our being affects all other aspects. It has been proven that there is a very strong connection between ignoring our emotions and physical disease.

We are also connected to everybody else because we all come from the same place and are made of the same thing—energy. This does not mean we have to like everyone else or agree with what others do, because we are all on individual journeys. But we are still connected. We are connected to animals, plants, trees, rivers, mountains, and the whole planet. Whatever we do to our animals and planet has consequences in other areas of nature because of this connection. When we talk of being mindful and whole, we are talking about becoming aware of this connection. Being kind to each other and animals and being thoughtful of our planet are so important.

What people need the most are support and encouragement. This is something that I have found is in short supply with many of my clients. I see people going through hard times, yet they have so much potential. They are highly intelligent, caring, generous, and creative people, yet they lack support and encouragement from those around them. When we endure difficult and challenging times, it is so important that we have people who are supportive and encouraging instead of those who ridicule, criticise, and tell us to just get over everything. Working in counselling, I see firsthand what a difference this can make in someone's life. We are not talking about fixing people's problems or living their lives for them. We are just talking about supporting them by being there for them, caring, and encouraging them.

As a man, I believe that my greatest demonstration of courage, strength, and achievement has been to confront my demons (issues and fears) and to accept that I have needed help and then ask for it. Commonly, men have not been associated with connecting with their emotions and especially asking for help. This is not a criticism, but denying our feelings is something society has encouraged for a very long time. When I was younger, I certainly had no intention of asking for help or even recognising that I needed it. Acknowledging, accepting, and then acting on this awareness has turned my life around. This is something everyone can do. Women also need to remember this. I want men to realise they do not need to suffer in silence. Part of being a man is using our courage and strength to confront, deal with, and grow from our problems.

Asking for help is not a sign of weakness but a sign of real strength. When you understand how wonderful life can be, you will never be afraid to ask for help again. This courage and strength are empowering and life-changing. Put your pride aside, and allow yourself to be human. Whether you are male or female, we are all here to help and be helped.

I will never try to be what other people want me to be. I will never try to be what society thinks I should be. I will stop judging myself for being human. I will release regrets from the past. I will be proud to express who I am freely and to give of myself freely. I accept love, peace, and abundance into my life because I deserve them. I look forward to discovering how much more I can experience and achieve. I will stop believing the illusions of the ego. Most of all, I am happy to be finally getting to know who I really am. Fifty-two years of life's lessons have not been wasted. Think outside the square because life is so much bigger and better than what you may expect.

Always ask for what you want. This is something many don't do. We can assume that people know what we want, we can expect that it will just happen, we can be afraid to ask for what we want, and we can justify why we shouldn't ask. Assuming is never a good idea in any part of life. Things rarely just happen without action, and being afraid to ask for what you want means there could be a problem with your self-esteem. Asking for what you want may not just be from a person; it could be from the universe. This is where meditation, affirmations, journaling, and positive self-talk come in.

I grew up being afraid to ask for anything. I was rarely offered anything, especially what I wanted. These days I am not afraid to ask, and I have so much more in my life. Asking is not being selfish if it is something that is important to you. It is a major part of communication, and communication is very healthy.

Time is very important. Time for yourself, your family, your friends, and time to experience life. Time is also an illusion. We believe we don't have enough of it, and it is going too fast. Life is about balance, so we have to make the most of our time and use it wisely. This means not sitting around, thinking how fast it is going. I see people rushing everywhere, especially on the road, and wonder why they are in such a hurry. Most people who rush around really don't have to. I believe this is one of the great illusions society has placed on us. The older I get, the less I tend to rush and want to be there five minutes sooner than everyone else or have to be first in line.

Don't be in a rush to get through life; life goes fast enough. You can't enjoy it when you are going flat out all the time. There are times when we need to move faster than others, but life is not meant to be a race. So slow down and enjoy it.

Those who win this time may not win next time. Those who lose this time may win next time. In my view, nobody is ever really a winner or a loser in life, because nobody can win all the time, and nobody is ever meant to keep losing. Winning and losing have nothing to do with who you are or your life. It is simply a representation of one experience that you have. To me, losing at a competition or failing an exam is simply a way of saying you need to try harder, increase skill level, or know more information. Winning is an achievement, and that is great. But it does not define you; it is not who you are. We can't win at something and say we have finally arrived and never have to try again.

I define a winner as someone who never stops trying, regardless of what is happening. A friend who died at a young age used to say to me that the only failure in life is the failure not to try. We are all winners.

Life requires us to feel our way through, not to see our way or to be told what to do. Seeing our way through is difficult because there are so many illusions, and it is easy to be deceived. Illusions come via the media, society, and the well-meaning opinions of others. Some of these illusions relate to our self-esteem and self-worth, so be careful about what you are taking on as a belief.

Feeling is the best way to be guided as to what we are doing right in life and what we may need to do differently. Your feelings don't deceive you, although we may not always understand what they are telling us. Validating is a good way to test our feelings, thoughts, and beliefs to see if they are real or just illusions. Write down a question, decision, or situation and draw two columns. One column will have reasons why something may be true, and the other column will have reasons why it may not be true. When we look at things on paper and really start asking questions, it is surprising what we find out. This has worked for me so many times as I have become older, and I know it can work for you.

Many people understand how to give love out but don't understand what it means to receive love. Therefore, they often don't. Signs that you are uncomfortable with receiving love can be finding it hard to accept a compliment, not allowing other people to emotionally or physically help you, having to please everyone else before yourself, never considering your own needs, justifying other people's poor treatment of you, hating the way you look, addiction, and sabotaging any chance of happiness when it comes along. I can honestly tell you that if you are not willing to receive love, you certainly won't. But you need to ask yourself, *Why?* You deserve love, and everyone needs to give and receive it. However, it has to start with you giving love to yourself.

One saying that we have in counselling is, "Fake it till you make it." Anytime we want to change something about ourselves or our lives, we need to start by making small steps toward that change. We often become overwhelmed with the enormity of the challenge and can easily give up. The idea behind faking it till you make it is to start placing positive energy behind your desire by visualising and feeling what you want to happen. Feeling and acting like the change has already happened creates a positive state. The energy, words, and thoughts help to reprogram your subconscious to make the changes manifest. Be like a child, and use your imagination to invent what you want. It really works.

As human beings, we often only see what we expect to see, hear what we expect to hear, and feel what we expect to feel. If we expect the best, there is no problem. However, if we expect the worst, there are plenty of problems. Our minds can become programmed to tunnel vision, and our perspectives become very narrow. It is vital that we learn to take in the big picture, and stop limiting our perceptions based on our past experiences or the views and opinions of others. We are all so capable of doing whatever we like, achieving our dreams, and experiencing happiness, joy, peace, and contentment.

We only use about 5 percent of our brains' potential. That percentage can be used to run a positive program. You are all incredible beings, and it is time to hold your heads up high, open your eyes, breathe deeply, and be proud of who you are. Take flight and expect the best.

Happiness is not a luxury; it is a birthright. Too many people believe they are meant to suffer or deserve to be punished. Nobody comes into this life being unworthy or second rate. Sometimes our experiences may make us believe that we do, but this is not true; it is merely an illusion. Everything becomes a habit or part of a cycle of thinking, and this may lead to distorted/dysfunctional beliefs. Nobody has ever been able to give me a valid reason for not being worthy or deserving unhappiness. Happiness, like everything, is a state of mind, so start thinking happy thoughts because you deserve to be happy.

We often underestimate the power of talking. So many people who are experiencing problems believe talking won't change anything, and what is done is done. The point here is that talking does change things in two ways. First, talking is an energy release. We are made of energy, so it is vital that we don't create an energy block. And second, talking helps us to make sense of things. When we stop and chat with someone, like a counsellor, we often hear ourselves differently and can say things that were previously unsaid. It helps to create a bigger and clearer picture. I have had this happen with many clients. It is good to be heard by someone who really cares.

It is not always about changing what has happened, but it can be about how to cope with what has happened in a more positive way. Don't bottle things up inside.

The people who make the most difference in the world are often the ones who don't know that they do. There are some very beautiful yet humble people who never realise the impact they have on others just by being themselves. This is something that can't be faked or imitated. It is a very natural part of who they are. Their smile and words alone can be enough to lift your spirits. These people don't have to pretend or be in the spotlight, because they are not self-centred or out for what they can get from others.

One thing I have realised on my journey through life is that it is the people behind the scenes who really make things happen. I know firsthand because I am married to one of them and also have them as family members and friends.

Sometimes the easy way is actually the hardest way. If we keep looking for the easy way out, we can avoid some major issues which, as long as we avoid them, won't go away. Some of these issues may surround avoiding confrontation, doing things because others want us to, never saying no, continuing addictions, staying in unhealthy relationships, and many other things that stop us from facing our problems. When we confront our issues, there may be some turmoil initially. However, we are actually making life much easier for ourselves in the long term.

The greatest discovery that I have made is that life has so much meaning. This is something I could never have said years ago. Over the years, there have been many tears and challenges and much confusion. But they have all made me stronger and have made me see who I really am. There is no better feeling than knowing you are doing what you are meant to be doing and sharing your life with people you love. My wife, Gail, highlights how much my life has turned around and that I am finally appreciating myself for who I really am. I am blessed more than I ever imagined with Gail, my family, friends, and clients. This is what life can hold for all of us if we are willing to confront the things that cause us pain. People who are willing to confront their pain often find purpose and meaning in unexpected ways. My wish is that you all find your true purpose and meaning.

Beware of the ego. Ego loves playing games with us by building on our insecurities and fears. Ego leads us to believe that we will never be good or worthy enough. Ego leads us to believe that we are what we own, what we do, what we look like, and what we achieve. Ego waits until we are at our weakest and then attacks with a barrage of negative thoughts. Ego wants us to feel superior to others and keeps us constantly striving for more.

I have been battling with my ego recently, and it is a great reminder that I have to be aware constantly. Believing in myself and what I do matters, and this brings me happiness. Having people I love in my life and good health matters. Not striving or competing with anyone else matters. Ego hates this sort of talk. Anytime that you find yourself feeling depressed or anxious, ego will be behind it. Ego has its purpose, but it is not to rule our lives. You are not your ego, and you have nothing to prove. You are good enough as you are, so be yourself and be happy.

We can never age too much as long as we stay young in our minds and hearts. Keeping fun and humour in our lives is so important. Having fun will keep you young in mind, body, and spirit. Fun is not just reserved for children; it is meant for everyone throughout their whole lifetimes. Fun is healing, and you can never do too much of what you enjoy. Many people can take life too seriously, which can cheat them out of happiness. In my opinion, how we age really has as much to do with our attitudes as it does with genetics or physical factors. Regardless of your age, physical limitations, or background, you still deserve to have fun and enjoy your life.

Passion is your intuition, your inspiration, your intention, your heart, your soul, and your strongest desires. When you are inspired by passion, you will never be deterred from your goals, and nothing nor nobody can discourage you. Passion says that this is you, and this is where you belong. This has nothing to do with anybody else; it belongs wholly to you. Passion is an important part of success and something never to be feared. Any strong, consistent feeling that won't go away and brings you to life is a sign of passion.

Passion doesn't have to be just associated with major goals. It can be something very simple. If you are not feeling passionate now, don't worry. Just relax, let go, and when the time is right, it will find you.

If we take the time to stop and think how far we have come, what we have been through, all the experiences we have had, and all of the obstacles we have overcome, we would be extremely proud. This is something that many of us don't do. I often hear people say they have done nothing special or have achieved nothing to be proud of. This is where feelings of unworthiness stem from. We simply don't acknowledge how special we are and the difference we make by just being in the world. We don't have to be an Albert Einstein or a Thomas Edison to be an achiever. Everyone I know has been through and achieved so much. Therefore, they can feel very proud of themselves. The change that I experienced when I realised what I have achieved and what sort of person I have become was monumental. When we realise how far we have come, we will realise how far we can go.

The calmest, most peaceful, and most tranquil place for us to go when we are stressed, anxious, or troubled is inside our minds and hearts. This place is available to us at all times and places. The value of meditation can't be underestimated in helping to achieve this. This has helped me to make many changes in my life. When we let everything from the outside world dictate our thoughts and feelings, we can become very overwhelmed with everything, and it may seem difficult to find answers. When we calm ourselves and look inwardly, the answers are there, and we can find peace. It is not a matter of escaping to some destination; it is a matter of getting to know yourself truly, realising that you are not your experiences, not your depression, or not your anxiety. You are your own safe haven that contains all of the answers you need. Being peaceful, happy, and tranquil is your natural state.

A happy thought has so much more power than an unhappy thought. Smiling takes far less energy than frowning. A good deed is far more rewarding than a bad one. Seeing a positive in someone or something will change your day for the better, unlike seeing the worst. Kind words have the power to heal rather than hurt, and love is a million times stronger than fear. Every day we have a choice as to how we look at things and how we would like to feel, regardless of what is happening, even though we may not think so. Choosing the right thought creates miracles and moves our lives forward in the right direction. The negative habits and cycles of the past can be broken and replaced with a brand-new, healthy way of life. The choice is yours.

Always be aware of your motivation for doing things. We have to be aware of our reasons for doing things, especially if we do not feel great about ourselves or our lives. We can do things to get back at someone, to prove something to someone else, to please someone else, to feel adequate, to get something from someone, for approval, for attention, and for many other unhealthy reasons. Healthy motivations include doing something because it is really what you want to do for yourself or to help someone else. If it is something you are passionate about or a part of your purpose, then that is positive and healthy. Your life is about you, so don't waste time being motivated by what other people want you to be or want from you.

Looking at what we can do for other people is so important. I believe life is about giving as much as you can whilst making sure your needs are met. When we give freely of our time, talents, gifts, skills, knowledge, love, and care, we are really living our purposes. As I always say, one's purpose has nothing to do with the job we do. It is the person we are. This gives a lot of meaning and quality to our lives, and at the same time, we enhance the lives of others. The more we give, the more we get back. When it is done for the right reasons, of course. Being a counsellor, I see the differences that caring and giving make.

My greatest transformation in life came when I saw past the pain and frustration of what happened to me in the past. I realised that I was not the difficult experiences of my past, the negative feelings that I had, or other people's opinions and judgements. There was an understanding that I was far more than what was happening to me.

It is easy to buy into the illusion of what we see. However, what we see is not always real. Knowing that we deserve only the best is crucial in transforming our lives. If you don't believe you deserve the best, ask yourself, Why? This is what I did, along with asking for help. When you believe you are good enough and deserving, everything will change.

Learning from other people's experiences and wisdom is wonderful, but never forget that what is right for them may not be right for you. It is really important that we don't live our lives by what other people think we should be doing or what they think is right for us. We can't judge ourselves based on their experiences. We are the only ones who can really know what we need. We may make mistakes, and often do, and this is our chance to gain our own wisdom and experience.

For a long time, I based my self-worth on the judgements of others, and I promise you it doesn't work. Other people can certainly help us, but they are not us. Each of us is here for our own journey, and it is up to us to work out how to complete it.

If people put you down, bully you, harass you, try to intimidate you, or anything that hurts your feelings, you have a choice. You can take it on and let them achieve their goal, or you can look past what is on the surface and pity them. When people need to do this to you, no matter what it is about, they are showing their own insecurities and lack of self-respect by trying to feel superior to you. These people are saying more about themselves than they are about you, even if they don't know it.

I have had this happen to me often in my life, and I used to buy into it. I was an easy target because of my low self-esteem. Well, times have changed. Since I have changed, these people don't come into my life anymore. The real me finally stood up. We are not talking about being aggressive, but we are talking about being assertive and strong. If you care about yourself, this sort of behaviour won't be tolerated. And when you do care about yourself, this sort of behaviour won't happen.

When I work with people, I often hear them say things like, "I have lost my strength," "I have lost my will," "I am not as strong as I used to be," and, "I don't have the courage." What I say to these people is, "You haven't lost these things, but you have temporarily misplaced them." We never lose the attributes of strength, will, courage, and determination. They are with us for life. Whether we use them or not is another matter. When we endure difficult times, we may feel that we have lost them. However, it is through these times that we use them the most. We use them because we are surviving. Feeling weak or lost does not make you a weak person; it's natural to feel this way in troubled times. I see people in tears, saying they can't cope or are not strong enough. Yet, they are coping, and they are strong enough. It takes some time and hard work, but believe me, we all have the strength, courage, will, and discipline that we not only need to survive but to progress and thrive.

One of the most important things for us to develop is self-respect. Self-respect will make our lives flow freely and with far more satisfaction. The essence of self-respect is loving ourselves unconditionally. Developing self-respect takes time, and it can challenge some long-held beliefs and thoughts. When we arrive at this point, we notice that we no longer need approval or acceptance from anyone, we will have more gratitude, we will honour everyone else's opinions without judgement, and, in turn, gain more respect from others. We find it is easier to forgive ourselves and others. We focus more on the good things in life.

Self-respect is not to be confused with pride or selfishness; they are nothing alike. Pride and selfishness are ego-driven. Self-respect is driven by our souls and born out of love.

We may think that we alone can't make a difference to the world, but this is not true. One person can and does make a difference to other people and life in general. When you are yourself and do kind acts, loving, helping, caring, listening, guiding, and anything that enhances somebody's day, you are making a difference. These acts do not have to be acknowledged or applauded. They don't have to be massive, but they do need to be meant in the right spirit with good intentions. The power of a good deed is far stronger than the power of a bad one, and that good deed radiates outwards to so many others. Remember that what we give out we get back. We underestimate the power we have, but I promise you that it is there. Our power radiates outwards like the rays of the sun.

Never underestimate the power of a compliment. Complimenting someone can make his or her whole day, whether it is someone you know or a complete stranger. This positive gesture can spread to other people throughout the day; this is known as the ripple effect. It is great for both the person giving and the one receiving the compliment. I never realised how many people never or rarely receive a compliment or positive feedback. This can be devastating for self-esteem and self-worth. I know some truly beautiful people who are rarely given a compliment, and this simply stuns me. Pay anyone that you care about a compliment, and help reassure them that they are loved and special. I would so much rather see something good in someone than something bad. The world needs more positivity.

Whenever I get scared or worry about something, I turn my focus back onto what I want to happen. Turning our focus to a positive helps break the cycle of anxiety and stress. This is very different from what I used to do. Previously, I would dwell on my fear, which eventually led me to a state of anxiety or anger. Focus plays a major role in the outcome of things. It may sound difficult, especially when we can't see how things will happen, but believe me it can be done. Thinking of what we want to happen, regardless of what appears to be happening, and looking at the positive ways we can make it happen are all likely to encourage a positive result. When we focus on what we want, we need to try to experience the feelings that you would be having with your desired outcome. Being grateful for what we have is also helpful in maintaining a positive focus. When things aren't going as we would like, it is easy to forget what we already have.

Going with the flow of life is much easier than pushing against it. Pushing against life means that we lack trust in ourselves and, therefore, in life itself. I believe we do this because we love to feel in control; we have to know when and how everything will happen. Human beings are the highest form of intelligence on the planet, yet we are the only ones that act this way. Animals, plants, and trees do not push against the flow of life or nature. They just go with it and do what they are meant to do.

I recently found myself falling back into the habit of going against the flow because I have allowed my ego to get in the way. I couldn't see the when or how, so I began doubting myself. Fortunately, I raised my awareness and did something about it. Even as a counsellor, I can still fall back into these patterns, so I need to work on myself constantly. We feel physically and mentally better when we go with the flow, so keep working on yourself.

Anger is something every person feels, yet it is really not understood. Most anger that we carry around is from early life experiences, such as not feeling loved, protected, nurtured, respected, or not being able to trust. As we grow up, we find different triggers that bring back anger. When we get angry as adults, we often act in a childish manner. In intimate relationships, anger is very symbolic because most of the things people argue about are not the real problem but symptoms of an underlying issue. Anger is a natural feeling and needs to be expressed in a healthy way. Otherwise, it can lead to physical illness.

The good news is that there are positive ways to deal with anger. We really need to find out what we are angry about and work through it so it does not become an issue that stops us from being happy and living fulfilling lives.

When we see the sun moving across the sky, we know it is an illusion, that it is really the earth moving around the sun, even though it gives the impression that it is the other way around. There are many illusions in life. We often accept them as being real. These include, "Nobody loves me," "I can't trust anyone," "People are out to get me," "Nothing ever goes right for me," "I am not a good person," "I am not as good as my siblings," "I am ugly," "I need to have more than others to be worthy," "I need a bigger house," "I have to put others' needs before my own," and "I need to fit in." These notions are not real no matter how real they seem. It is just like the sun moving across the sky.

Seeing through these illusions is a challenge for all of us because we have developed so much fear. This is where counselling can play a major role. We need to look inside ourselves to discover how our illusions began. It is difficult, but it can be done. Seeing through the illusion allows you to know your real self and live the life you really want and truly deserve.

For so long I believed that I would never find a special relationship. Having had a partner die and having been in dysfunctional relationships, I wasn't sure if there was something wrong with me or if I was just unlucky. It turned out to be neither. However, there were reasons for what I had been through. Not understanding, appreciating, respecting, or loving myself was the problem. Once I began addressing these issues, my life changed dramatically.

It is hard to imagine how I felt back in those days because it seems like an eternity ago. Having met my beautiful wife, Gail, is my reward for anything bad that has ever happened in my life. This is the relationship I always dreamed of having. Gail is the most wonderful, caring, beautiful, and selfless person I have ever met. She appreciates and accepts me for who I am; she takes care of me like I could never have imagined. We are connected to each other on so many levels. And I can honestly say that not even love describes how I feel about her. I would change nothing in my past because it brought us together.

Never give up on your dreams. Remember that if you are looking for love, you must begin by loving yourself.

I talk to a lot of people who believe they don't have a purpose in life. They also think they don't make a difference. I can honestly say that every single person on the planet does have a purpose and does make a difference. Having a purpose does not necessarily relate to the work you do. It does not relate to our achievements or social statuses. It has nothing to do with any of these things. Purpose is really about being the person you were meant to be, following your dreams, the experiences that you have, and the experiences that you create for others. It is not being afraid to be yourself, express yourself, believe in yourself, and love yourself. It is being the best person you can be, rising to your full potential, and making the world a better place because you are here. When we work on these areas, we will know our purpose and understand the difference we make.

Acceptance is a very important part of any healing work. There are so many people who try to live in denial. They find so many ways to distract themselves from the real issues. This could be through working too hard or addiction. It may be involving themselves in the lives of others, so they don't have to think about their own lives. This is not meant to be judgemental because I have done this myself and realise how easy it is to do. Most times we are not even aware that we are doing it. Deep down we always know if something feels right. Believe me, ignoring issues and pretending everything is good will not change anything.

There are steps we can take to begin the healing process. Acknowledgement (being honest with yourself), acceptance (commitment to healing), and asking for help are good ways to start. The thing that finally helped me to accept myself was accepting the fact that I was not happy with how my life was going.

People who are perfectionists will always struggle to be happy because we simply can't be perfect at everything all the time. This was never meant to be the case for human beings. We are already perfect in our hearts and souls. But the human experience means that we have to make mistakes and have times where we don't perform as well as we could. This is how we learn. Please don't beat yourself up over being human because you will only make yourself miserable. Perfectionists are likely to suffer from stress and anxiety, which can lead to ongoing physical problems.

Life has a way of forcing us to confront things; these days more than ever. Ignoring problems will not make them go away; it only makes them worse. Those who try to distract themselves from their issues only make their lives harder. Some may distract themselves with addictions, work, or denial.

For most of my life I lived in denial about so many things because I either had no idea how to handle them, or I pretended they did not exist. This only caused me more pain. Today I know the only way to resolve things is to confront them. Otherwise, life may do it in a less than subtle way. We all have the strength to do this even if it means asking for help. I will never be afraid to ask for help again.

The three hardest things for people to say are, "I am sorry," "I love you," and, "I need help." These are all things we need to or want to say at times. However, for some reason, we may feel unable to do so. All these things can make us feel weak or vulnerable, yet there is absolutely no reason to believe this. As human beings, we all need to say these things at some stage. Pride is an absolutely massive obstacle in this process. Pride can keep us lonely, depressed, angry, and stressed. Being human means that we make mistakes, we need help from other people, and, of course, we love other people. Never be afraid to say any of these things. They can only help you to enhance your life and the lives of others.

Having a broken heart is one of the worst feelings there is. There is no easy way to go through this experience. It is painful. Looking back at some of my experiences in this area, I remember feeling as though it would be impossible for me to ever be happy again. At times, there were intense sadness and feelings of desperation. What we need to remember is that it is not meant to be a pleasant experience; it is a learning experience. We need to be extremely patient with ourselves whilst we take the time to deal with it, understand it, and eventually prosper from it.

One of the lessons I learned from heartbreak was that I don't ever want to be with someone who doesn't feel the same way about me. Today I can honestly say that I am so grateful for these experiences because they led me to true happiness. If not for these times, I would not have met the perfect person for me, I would not be doing the career that I love, and I would certainly not love myself. There is a reason for everything—however hard it may be to see at the time—and it is never too late to find true happiness.

The human body is made of pure energy. This is exactly what we are in our most basic form. Everything in life is made of energy. Our emotions are energy in motion, our thoughts are energy, and our words have energy connected with them. The entire planet is made up of the same energy. It stands to reason that we are all affected by each other's energy, and this is exactly what happens. This is why it is so important to surround yourself with the right people, have a good diet, and live and work in a good atmosphere.

This, of course, does not always happen, especially in work environments. When we are with negative people or in negative environments, our energy levels become depleted. This is when we can be prone to depression, exhaustion, lethargy, and sickness. Thinking negative thoughts will attract more negativity because like attracts like. It is important to remember the role that energy plays in life, so we can learn to influence life in a positive way.

There are some things we often say that come very naturally but are not very helpful. "Should" is one of the worst. The word "should" is very judgemental. It implies that we are wrong or not good enough. This word can be replaced by the word "could," which says maybe we did not make the best decision this time, but it is okay, and we will learn from the experience for next time. It is a forgiving word.

"If only" is also not very helpful or healthy. It will keep you living in the past and caught up in regret. It has no real meaning because it did not happen, and, therefore, there is something we need to learn from the situation. This can be replaced with, "I now understand," which means you accept the situation. It eventually leads to a better outcome next time.

Another saying is, "I have to," which draws us away from taking responsibility and makes us believe we have no control over our lives. People often say this when they don't really have to but may feel obliged to. This could be replaced with "I choose to." This is more accurate.

All these words may seem insignificant. But when we say something hundreds of times, it can have a very negative effect on our states of mind.

One common problem people face is procrastination. We may have some brilliant ideas or some unique talents, skills, and dreams. However, they may never come to life because we simply can't make a decision to do anything about them. Fear is a major contributor to this. What if it doesn't work? What if I look foolish? What will other people say? It probably won't work. Others have tried and failed. There is a list of excuses that goes on and on. We can find ourselves looking at every reason why something can't happen instead of why it can.

Every good idea needs action to follow it through. I believe that if your dream, desire, or idea is strong enough, it is essential that you try. One thing people will never be able to say about me when I am gone is that I died wondering. Have a go because there is nothing to lose and everything to gain.

Some good questions to ask yourself:

What am I really scared of?

What is it that is stopping me from achieving?

What is it that I really want?

Why can't I move ahead?

Why am I afraid of feeling?

What would make me happy?

Who am I?

What is stopping me from being me?

What is the worst that can happen?

These are all good questions because they make us think about life and question what is happening in ours. They can raise awareness to where we are as individuals. Many of us don't ask ourselves these questions, but they can be so helpful by making us look at the big picture of our lives. Begin to question yourself because you may get to know yourself better.

Do not be afraid to feel. This can relate to any feeling, negative or positive. This is one thing I have observed over many years. So many of us try not to feel, which can be a recipe for disaster. It can be due to denying negative feelings like sadness, anger, disappointment, frustration, guilt, and resentment. It can also be denying positive feelings like not allowing yourself to feel love or get too close to someone in case you get hurt. Some may not allow themselves to get too excited when something good happens because they are waiting for something bad to even it up.

Feelings and emotions are the guidance system for our lives, and it is essential that we acknowledge and express them—in a healthy way, of course—if we are to be happy. If we are afraid of feeling, we are afraid of opportunity, possibility, and our true potential. Feel and be free.

Affirmations work really well if they are used correctly and with the right attitude. An affirmation needs to be a positive statement and said in the present tense, or said as an intention. Some good affirmations could be, "I have perfect health," "I am really happy with my body," "I have great fitness and vitality," and "I always find helpful and attentive people to serve me." Some not so good affirmations could be, "I will lose weight," "I will get fit," "I will stop smoking," and, "I will try to control my anger." With the first examples, we are saying them as though they have already happened; we are making positive statements. The second examples say they will happen in the future. Therefore, they will always be in the future and will never happen now. The second group of examples also have negativity attached to them because they imply you are not perfect right now. This, in turn, implies that you are judging yourself on your body and not on who you really are.

The other thing with affirmations is that your thoughts and words need to be consistent. It is no good saying affirmations twenty times in the morning and twenty times in the evening if you spend the rest of the day saying and thinking negative thoughts in between your affirmations. The affirmation should also be said with real feeling, as though you have already achieved your desired outcome. Affirmations have real power if used correctly.

Friends are so important. Real friends who are there for you in the good times and the bad times, friends who don't try to control or manipulate you, friends who listen to you and accept you for who you are. Friends who do not judge you for your opinions and beliefs. Real friends don't have to be with you all the time. But when they are with you, it is quality time. I have seen many one-sided friendships over the years, and they are not healthy. Gail and I are so blessed to have so many wonderful and true friends in our lives.

Another good thing to remember about friendship is that you have to be your own best friend. Nobody knows you as well as you know yourself, and nobody knows what is best for you like you do. You come into this life with yourself, and you will leave with yourself. You are the common theme. If you can't be your own best friend, there are issues that need to be worked on.

When I talk of love, I always refer to unconditional love, for this is the only real love. So many people struggle to find this in relationships because they can't find it in themselves. They criticise themselves, carry unnecessary guilt, have distorted beliefs and negative self-talk, compare themselves with others, and many more self-sabotaging behaviours. This was me for much of my life. How can we expect unconditional love from another person if we don't give it to ourselves? How can we give it to someone else if we don't have it within us? When you look in the mirror, see past the reflection and look deep into your eyes. See the beautiful soul and the beautiful heart that is the real you. We are not our bodies, we are not our minds, and we are not the opinions or judgements of other people. We are all special and deserving beings.

Don't let the enormity of a task discourage you from trying to achieve your goals. Sometimes we try to look too far ahead at something we are trying to achieve, and it can seem overwhelming. This has happened to me on many occasions. I know so many people who have given up on their dreams because it all seemed way too hard. This can also apply to things that we have to do or not want to do, such as dealing with grief or attending to legal and family affairs. What I have come to realise is that the best way to approach a problem or goal is to do it one step at a time. If we look too far ahead, a task may appear too difficult. It is necessary to have a strong desire and plan as much as you can, but most of all, take it one step at a time. Break it down into smaller manageable stages, and tackle it piece by piece. Try to do something every single day, no matter how small, toward your goals and dreams, and they will happen.

The greatest work we do is not what we do at our jobs but what we do as people. Often we are judged by the kind of work we perform. However, that is not a good description of who we really are. What we do as people, how we treat others, the joy we bring to others, and the difference that we make to the world by being the unique person we are is what life is all about. Offering kindness, compassion, understanding, and humour can be life-changing for everyone. This is something I wish I understood growing up. We all have something very valuable to contribute to life, so never underestimate yourself and the unique contribution you make to the world.

Never be afraid to accept a compliment or kind gesture from someone you know means well. People struggle with this concept usually because deep down, they do not truly believe they are worthy of it. Never forget that you are worthy and deserving. When you can accept these gestures graciously, you send a positive message into your subconscious mind, which will help to raise your self-esteem. You are also helping the person offering the compliment or gesture by giving him or her the opportunity to do something nice. I certainly love to give compliments and let people know they are appreciated, and it feels great when they accept your kind gesture.

Nobody can ever make us feel what we are not already willing to feel about ourselves. How many times do we allow the judgements, criticisms, or opinions of others to hurt us? I grew up believing what other people thought of and said about me. Nothing else has created so much chaos in my life as this thought process. We are not what other people think of us. If other people's comments hurt us, it must reflect how we feel about ourselves on the inside. When we develop true self-love, it is impossible to be hurt by the opinions of others. Other people can't really know us like we know ourselves, so what gives them the right to judge us? Have they walked in our shoes?

People who develop self-love are self-assured, they don't need approval from others, they have charisma, and they are great to be around. And all they do is share their love with those who appreciate it. They have a certain quality because they have taken the time to get to know themselves on a deeper level. If you allow others to form your opinion of yourself, you may need to do some serious self-esteem work. Love who you are, and others will love you for who you are as well.

When we experience any painful event, we experience grief. The death of someone close, the ending of a relationship, loss of a job, physical or mental trauma, and many other difficult experiences are all forms of grief. Grief is the most difficult thing for humans to experience. However, it is through these experiences that many people find their greatest courage, strength, and faith. Painful experiences are our greatest teachers, as difficult as they are. They provide the opportunity to really grow and learn more about ourselves and life. We gain perspective. The closing of one chapter leads to the opening of a new one.

Grief takes time to deal with, and we need to be patient with ourselves and others. Grief is a very individual and personal experience, so don't judge yourself on how other people experience their grief. There is no right or wrong way to grieve, and there is no set time to grieve. My own grief experiences have made me who I am today and given me a truly amazing life. If you are suffering with grief, talk to someone. Don't suffer in silence.

Each day I wake up is a gift because I am still alive. Each new day is a new opportunity to create exactly what I want in my life, even if it takes a little while. Each new day is another chance to share my life with those I love. Each new day gives me the opportunity to do the work I love, counselling. Each new day I am grateful for what I have because I have the opportunities many don't have.

Gratitude is a wonderful way to create more of what you would like in your life. Life is wonderful and a very precious gift, so enjoy.

One of the most powerful emotions is sadness. If I think of the role sadness has played in my life, I can honestly say it has taught me more than any other emotion. It forced me to look at my life in so many ways. Whilst it is a difficult emotion to experience, it awakens us to what we need to see in ourselves. It made me aware of past issues that were still haunting me and of my insecurities. It made me analyse my dysfunctional beliefs and encouraged me to finally be honest with myself. When I decided to deal with my sadness, I found it very healing and cleansing. If I had never let my sadness in, I would not be so happy now. Like all emotions, sadness needs to be acknowledged and expressed. Any emotion need not be feared, as they are necessary parts of who we are. If we are in touch with our emotions, we are in touch with ourselves and life in general.

Life is not a destination but the greatest journey of all. We can choose to be merely a passenger who watches life go by. Someone who is controlled and manipulated by others; who live their lives for everyone but themselves; who is cheated, abused, and criticised; and who is always accepting second best. In other words, a victim.

On the other hand, we can choose to get in the driver's seat and take command of our lives. We can be responsible, assertive, proud, and direct our lives where we want them to go. We can be in charge of our lives and excited by all the possibilities and opportunities that come our way. We can experience life to the full, and this is exactly how it is meant to be. When we live this way, we can give more love and care to others because we are giving to ourselves. This is not being selfish, but it is self-care, which I always speak about. Life always has challenges, but we have the strength to overcome them. Life is the greatest journey and experience there is. There is no dress rehearsal, so live life to the full because you do have a choice.

There are a lot of people who struggle with saying no. They are always helping others, doing favours, sorting out others' problems, doing the majority of the work, and forgoing their needs for others' without getting anything in return. These are what I refer to as serial givers, and I used to be one of them. Helping others is great and something I love to do. But we have to understand that we can't always be the one doing the giving; it is not healthy.

Serial givers attract serial takers. This is especially true in relationships. We have a duty to ourselves to make sure our needs are met first and that we make our lives our priority. We can always help others more when we are taking care of ourselves, whether it is in an emotional or practical sense. Do not become the one who is always taken advantage of. Life needs to work both ways, and every adult needs to take responsibility for their own lives. Help and support as much as you can, but remember that you are your first priority. And if you are physically and emotionally healthy, you can be of more help to others. It is okay to say no.

One night about eight years ago I was sitting up at one of my favourite lookout points in Adelaide. I was wondering what was wrong with me after the ending of another relationship, no job, and little money. There was a knowing that I had done the right thing by ending my relationship, but there was a lot of sadness and grief surrounding the situation. The realisation came to me that if I gave half of the love to myself that I gave to others, my life would be very different. It was apparent that I had become a serial giver. Givers attract takers. This is not a criticism of my former partners, because I was allowing this to happen. They were my teachers. This had happened in all areas of my life, not just intimate relationships. It was like I had such a need to be accepted that I tried to win people over by giving all I had. That night I made a deal with myself that I would not allow this to ever happen again. I decided to give love to myself and care for myself as I did for others. I was now being true to myself.

Since that night, I met my perfect match, my wife, Gail, who is more wonderful and giving than words can say. I have also attracted all good people into my life and started my own business. I still give, but I am given to as well. Love starts with the self.

Inside all of us lives a small child. A child who likes to have fun, be excited, gets scared, and needs comfort and reassurance. This child often comes out to play when we are having troubled times as adults. We can often revert to childish behaviour in the form of tantrums, blaming, running away, and sulking. The important thing to know is that we all carry around all our experiences somewhere in our subconscious minds. When there is a trigger, it can bring back old feelings and memories; this is completely natural. No matter how old we get, we all still like to have our childhood needs of love and nurturance fulfilled. It is important to recognise this need in ourselves and to do something about it if it is causing us problems. No childhood is perfect, and we need to be aware of the effect our childhoods have on us.

Unfulfilled needs of love and nurturance explain why so many people end up in dysfunctional relationships, suffer addictions, and go into self-sabotaging behaviour. Love yourself, and keep nurturing the child inside you.

One thing I like to teach my clients is to focus on themselves and not their problems. This is because we are not our problems. However, we always have the answers to our problems inside us. We have to accept and understand our problems, but if we focus on the problem itself, it can consume us. Doing things like meditation, yoga, exercise, or even just spending some quiet time relaxing are great ways to get in tune with yourself. If you focus on what is happening inside you with your feelings and thoughts, you are more likely to gain clarity and direction. It is a better way to get to know the real you and understand how to solve your problems and achieve the life that you desire. It doesn't matter if it takes a bit of time.

Life is perfection, and we are perfection because we are a part of life. There is nothing to prove, and nothing that has to be achieved apart from seeing and realising your own perfection. We are all on different journeys with different experiences, which makes life interesting. However, these experiences do not define us as people. We are all expressions of love, and love is what defines us, regardless of our experiences.

I see so many people looking for love outside themselves, and this always leads to disappointment. Looking for love on the inside is a necessary step to finding love on the outside. The day you see this perfection and love in yourself will be the day you finally believe in miracles.

Showing gratitude for what we have is an important step in attracting more of what we want. It is easy to focus on what we don't have or what is not happening. This is more likely to block what we want. What we focus our attention on we tend to attract, so we have to be careful about what we are thinking and saying. Each day I start by being grateful for my life, everybody in it, my health, and everything that I have.

Too often I see people who have so much, yet they don't see it. They concentrate on wanting more and more and are not grateful for what they already have, no matter what it is. I have been guilty of this in the past, but as I grow older, I see so much to be grateful for, especially the really important things—life, family, friends, health, this beautiful planet, and wisdom.

Domestic violence is not just about physical abuse. Domestic violence covers mental and emotional abuse as well, and this can be equally if not more devastating than physical abuse. There are no scars or bruises to hide, but the damage is severe. When a partner is being overly critical, demanding, controlling, manipulative, sarcastic, and intimidating, it signals domestic violence. Partners who tolerate this form of abuse will have very low self-esteem and no self-worth. They are insecure and seek to fill a void in their lives. They believe any love is better than no love. Make no mistake: anybody who is abusive in this way does not love you.

Partners who inflict this violence are also insecure and have low self-esteem. They seek to fill a void in their lives through domination and control. This is a major problem in our society, and it is time to educate people about it. Nobody deserves this treatment.

One thing I have found very helpful in changing my life is taking responsibility. Responsibility is not about who or what is right or wrong. It is about realising that we have choices, and those choices have consequences. Sometimes the choices are not easy, but they are still choices. This takes away from the blame game, which does nothing but cause more sorrow. Everything that happens to us is there to teach us and make us wiser.

Recognising that as adults our choices are our responsibilities is important and empowering. Taking responsibility, even when you have been wronged, gives you control over your life and helps to build a brighter future. Responsibility stops you from being a victim, and, therefore, you become empowered.

The process of change always starts on the inside. If you look outside yourself to create positive changes, you will be waiting forever. Many people think their lives will be different if they find a partner or a different partner, if they had more money, if they had a different job, if they had a better body, if they are not cheated by a business partner, and many other excuses that can explain why they are not where they want to be. The only place change begins is on the inside with your beliefs, thoughts, and words. Everything that goes wrong outwardly in life is really a reflection of what is happening on the inside. Therefore, we must work from the inside out. When we work on self-esteem, self-worth, and self-love, we will see changes in every aspect of our lives. You have control over any form of change you want to occur if you look in the right place.

Most of the problems we experience as adults are due to unresolved grief. Grief is not just about losing a loved one. It is also about the ending of any significant phase of life. The ending of one phase of life signals the beginning of a new one. Grief can occur through the loss of a relationship, loss of employment, moving, retirement, experiencing illness or injury, children leaving home, and many more things. We can grieve for things that may not have happened as well, like not finding the right partner, not having children, or not following a desired career path.

Grief is present in many more forms than we may think, but it is rarely thought of as such. Unresolved grief can lead to anger, resentment, guilt, sadness, addiction, depression, and anxiety. It can derail our lives completely if we allow it. It is vital that we address our grief, or it can consume us. Grief is a natural part of life and can be dealt with, so don't be afraid to ask for help.

We tend to be in a rush to make everything happen these days. The age of instant gratification leads to more depression and anxiety, in my opinion. If we stop and think about it, what is the rush? Life needs to be appreciated, and we can only appreciate life when we live in the moment. When we are rushed, stressed, and anxious, we can't be in the moment. This leads us to not appreciating what we have and what life is about. Things like taking the time to get to know someone in a relationship, waiting until you can afford a better car or bigger home, being patient for that job opportunity, and always making time for yourself are things that seem to have faded out of awareness. Being in a rush can also lead to making poor decisions. We can miss out on so many of life's simple pleasures when we are always in a rush. It is great to have dreams and goals. However, they take time and work to make them manifest, and that can be half the fun. Don't rush and miss out on living.

Being intelligent is not merely about a high IQ. Plenty of people with high IQs are very unhappy, lonely, frustrated, and socially challenged. Intelligence is about a combination of IQ and, more important, being emotionally intelligent. It is a fact that people with emotional intelligence, who may also have high IQs, are more successful than those with just high IQs.

Emotions are a part of us and an essential part of life, not optional extras. It is emotional intelligence that gives wisdom, knowledge, and power, and these are essential ingredients for happiness. Understanding your emotions brings you closer to understanding yourself and, therefore, to what makes you happy. This is why I believe our educational system needs to take a closer look at making emotional intelligence a subject in school.

People often think they don't have a choice, but they do. The choice may not be an easy one, but there is still a choice. Sometimes, we have to make a choice that has no easy answer and will lead to short-term pain no matter what we decide. However, if it is for long-term benefit, it is probably a choice worth making. I have been in this situation, and it is difficult. But the benefits I am seeing today made it all worthwhile.

Choices and decisions—whether major or minor ones—will always be a part of life. Most important, always remember that you have a choice. If you make a wrong one, learn from it, so it doesn't happen again. Realising we have a choice can be very empowering, and it also reminds us that we do have control over our lives.

Having dreams and wishes is really important, but they need action to make them happen. Saying we want something but only ever talking about it or coming up with every reason under the sun why it can't happen is something I am sure we have all done. Even taking one small step every day toward your dream will help it to come true. But if you want something to happen, your words, thoughts, and actions have to be in harmony with your desires. Things don't happen without action no matter how much we wish and dream. There is no time like today to place your excuses aside, and start making your dreams a reality.

The capacity of the human spirit is amazing. We have so much strength and determination to achieve amazing goals. This is obvious when we see what people have achieved after suffering severe physical or emotional traumas. People find incredible strength to not only cope but to succeed and prosper. Imagine if we used that strength and determination in our everyday lives. Imagine if we did not have to go through traumas to find our true potentials. We can turn our lives into whatever we want them to be because we have the ability and spirit to accomplish anything. Desire, spirit, and ability equal success.

Those that wish to control, manipulate, and ridicule can't be in a loving relationship as these things are totally the opposite of love. The reasons for this sort of behaviour is usually a lack of love for themselves and an intense fear of being alone. They become the classic bully. They prey on people they perceive to be weak and helpless. It is a game that has gone on since the beginning of time. It is not up to anybody else to help them if they are not willing to admit they need help. Building your own self-love, self-esteem, and self-worth is the best way to ensure you are not on the receiving end of this behaviour.

If we hear things often enough, we can begin to believe them. Whether they are true or false is irrelevant. When we hear negative things on a regular basis, we can begin to accept them as being the truth. We can have a lot of unhealthy beliefs living in our subconscious minds, and the more we hear negative comments, the more real they seem. This has happened to me, and I see it happening to so many. Today, the thought of taking on somebody else's negative opinion of me is absolutely ridiculous.

Other people can criticise or ridicule us, and we can also do this to ourselves via negative self-talk. The words we speak and the thoughts we think have power, so if we speak and think negatively, we will create negative outcomes. The criticisms and opinions of other people belong to them, not you, so choose not to take them on. Enter a brand-new program into your mind that is full of positive statements and thoughts. Choose to think the best.

Releasing expectations is a good way to avoid disappointment. So many times in the past I have built up expectations only to be disappointed. This comes from a rigid way of thinking that has placed many limitations on my life. There are no guarantees in life, and it is vital that we keep an open heart and open mind. The good thing to know is that through some of my earlier disappointments have come some of my greatest blessings and achievements. Expect good things in your life, but we have to be flexible about how things will happen because good things often come in unexpected ways. Stay in the moment, enjoy the moment, and be open to what life can offer.

Being stubborn is not just about having a rigid attitude we are not willing to bend on. Being stubborn can be refusing to see what is right in front of our eyes, something that is obvious or thinking that we will make something work when it is quite obvious it won't. I used to be very confused about being stubborn. I thought I was the least stubborn person in the world because I always did what everybody else wanted me to do. Realisation finally set in when I realised I was keeping myself stuck in the same situations because I refused to admit I had issues to deal with. This is common with intimate relationships, and relationships showed me how stubborn I was being. Life is too short to keep living in dysfunctional ways, so open your eyes, be willing to admit that you need to change, and start making changes.

Others may not always understand you or share your opinion, and that is okay. The important thing is that you understand yourself and the reasons for the choices you make. It is important to become aware of our reasons and motivations for doing what we do—the reasons we enter into a relationship, make a certain career choice, prioritise the way we do, and the image we display to other people. Being yourself is so important. We really need to get in touch with who we are. Then we will know what will truly make us happy. Being happy has nothing to do with anyone else or their priorities and desires.

It is essential that we start living in the moment, the here and now. The past has been an experience to teach us. We learn from it whether it has been good or bad. The future has yet to be written. It is in the moment that we have the power to influence the future. The present moment is where we have power and control over our lives. Living in the past is not healthy; neither is living too far in the future. Life is happening right now, so pay attention to what is happening for you and how you feel right now. This will guide you to where you need to be to create the future you desire.

Holding onto bitterness and resentment hurts only one person—you. It can't possibly change things or affect the person you are angry with. The keys to moving ahead and finding peace and happiness are to forgive, let go, and focus on yourself. This sounds difficult to do because it is human nature to want to find so-called justice, retribution, or revenge. When you go down this path, you are actually attracting the opposite energy from what you want, and you are still not healing the past. It is a losing situation. Believe me, there is nothing to be gained by holding onto a grudge except to block your own happiness. Learn to focus on yourself and the life that you desire, not on the past or people who have wronged you. Good feelings attract happiness.

There are no shortcuts to achieving satisfying goals. Every significant goal you set for yourself has to have challenges and obstacles to be overcome, or they would not mean as much. Anything that is a worthy goal deserves and requires hard work and effort. I believe the real feeling of success comes from, not finally achieving the goal, but from the feeling of knowing how much work and effort you have done to make it happen. If things were handed to you on a plate, they would mean nothing, and you would not appreciate it. You would not gain anything from it.

Never give up on your goals no matter what obstacles are in your way. You deserve the feeling of success that comes with your hard work, endeavours, and achievements.

I believe that two major blockages for people in finding happiness are trust and faith. The problem is we have to find these things in ourselves before we can feel them with other people and life in general. We can have our trust and faith eroded by difficult life experiences, especially in childhood. These experiences do not have to affect the rest of our lives.

Without trust and faith, we expect the worst to happen and will look for negativities in the majority of situations, which are then likely to manifest. Trust and faith are all about building self-esteem and valuing and accepting yourself with all your faults. It is looking beyond the surface and all of the ego-dominated ways of society.

Happiness and contentment are the best feelings we can have. But do you know what is it that makes you happy? If you are always striving for more and more to make yourself happy, you will be very disappointed. Money, material gain, and status will not necessarily deliver happiness and contentment. Showing appreciation for what you do have and being content with the important things of life will attract more abundance for you in all areas of your life. Having love, kindness, family, friends, and health as priorities in your life will allow you to live a life that is meaningful and with far less stress and anxiety. Enjoy the experience of life for what it is—a gift.

Attitude is so important for living a happy life. A positive attitude can't stop difficult things from happening, but it will heavily influence the outcome for the future. A positive attitude is the major difference between people who are happy and successful and those who are not. In life we get what we focus on, and if our attitudes are negative, we will get back more negativity.

Be careful to note what your attitude is toward yourself, others, and life in general. Your attitude really does have enormous power.

Love crosses all boundaries and is in all forms. Time, distance, and circumstance have no bearing on unconditional love. Love is always present and is contained in every living thing and every space. Love can't die because it is infinite, a never-ending story. Love knows no fear or ridicule. Love is responsible for all healing, happiness, contentment, peace, and joy. Think about how powerful love is, and remember that you are a living representation of pure love. When you understand this, you will be creating miracles in your own life.

Many often wonder what the meaning of their lives is, so I will share mine with you. The meaning of my life, as I see it, is to realise my full potential as a human being. This means seeing the true love that is just me without anybody or anything else. Embracing my faults and weaknesses as well as my strengths. The true love that says I am good enough because I am here.

The other part of my meaning is to share my knowledge and wisdom with others so that they may find their meanings and happiness as well. What I have learned over the years is worth sharing, and this is why I have chosen a career in counselling and self-development.

Self-doubt is created in many ways. One of the most common is to be repeatedly told something negative about yourself. This can happen in unhealthy relationships and through bullying at school and work. If you are willing to believe what others say about you, the cycle will never end. What others say to you says far more about them than you. They are talking about their insecurities and weaknesses. They have low self-esteem, so they try to bring you down to make themselves feel better.

Nobody can make us believe anything we are not already willing to believe. Nobody has the right to put you down or criticise you. Believe in yourself.

When teaching and guiding young children, it is important to remember that teaching is not just telling or showing them what to do. It is about leading by example. Children take in everything that happens, including how we interact with each other, how we handle problems, and every other aspect of us. Their brains are like sponges, and they absorb information easily. They also absorb the atmosphere they live in. Between the ages of birth and five years old is a very important time for children. This is the foundation for the rest of their lives. It is important that they develop a solid foundation and feel secure. This is the best gift you can give them.

One of the greatest motivators in the world is fear. Advertising companies thrive on using fear to sell products and services. Fear affects all of us and is one of our biggest challenges in life. It can be fear of what will happen or fear of what won't happen. All fear is simply fear of the unknown. The thing to remember is that there is no courage without fear, there is no achievement without fear, and there is no learning or wisdom without fear. If we let fear dictate the terms of our lives, we will be very limited and unhappy. Fear is something to embrace and use to your advantage. Fear is natural and healthy, so start to control your fear instead of it controlling you.

Anytime I have achieved something it has been when I had a strong passion accompanied by a knowing it would happen. This knowing is hard to describe, but it is very real. It is accompanied by constant dreaming and thinking of what I love and seeing myself doing it, being there, or being with someone. In my childhood, I was terrible at school. I hated studying, I hated school, and I was timid and shy with no confidence. Yet growing up, I also had a vivid imagination and goals.

My first significant goal was getting a job at the airport because of my passion with flying and aeroplanes. It took six years, but I got the job. Next was learning to fly. After securing my job at the airport, I financed my own flying lessons and gained my commercial pilot's licence. Then there was going overseas, gaining my counselling diploma, starting my business, and most of all, meeting my wife. All of this achieved by someone who was rated as a poor student and had no confidence. Passion and intention can make anything happen regardless of what you have been told or past experiences.

Every single time in my life when I have felt hurt or down, discouraged, or hopeless, there has always been someone there to help me. There has never been a time when I have been totally alone and abandoned, even in my darkest hours. This help does not always come from who you may expect or in the way we imagine, but it is always there. Whenever I have had doubts about life, someone has turned up out of nowhere, or something has happened to make me change my mind.

Things don't always work out the way we plan, but I believe that when we need help, it is always there. This may involve admitting you need help and actively seeking it out. Keeping an open heart and mind is essential to receiving the help you need.

If you miss an opportunity today, don't worry. Look for another one tomorrow. Opportunity is around us constantly. However, we only see opportunity if we are open and receptive to it. I know I have missed opportunities because of being negative, having tunnel vision, and just being stressed about things. Excessive worry, trying too hard, and listening to other people's negativities are great ways to miss an opportunity.

The world works in mysterious ways, and we can make it work for us or against us. Important to remember is the fact that opportunity does not always come in the form we are expecting. It can sneak in the back door. Trust and belief in yourself are vital if you are to recognise opportunity when it comes.

Raising awareness is essential for all of us. We need to understand how we create the events in our lives, how we get caught up in cycles and habits, our thoughts and feelings, who we are and our purposes, how life works, and that there is far more to life than what we can see, hear, and feel with our senses. A lack of awareness is largely responsible for creating every problem we have in our lives. Lack of awareness creates every turmoil in the world.

When we work on creating awareness, our physical health, mental health, and prosperity will all start to improve. There are many steps we can take to start doing this. Counselling, meditation, yoga, exercise, reading self-development books, and making time for yourself are all important in raising awareness.

Even negative feelings have a purpose. We often think we should not get negative or feel down. These feelings are a completely natural part of life, and they do serve a purpose. They tell us that we need to do something differently, look at something in a different way, or that there is something we need to pay attention to. They guide us. Without these feelings, we would not learn anything and would not be able to appreciate what we have.

One problem with these feelings is that we can get used to having them and then stay locked in a cycle of negativity that can lead to long-term depression or anxiety. We need to work on ourselves when we feel down. But remember that it is natural to get this way at times, and it is just another opportunity for growth and learning.

Sometimes we can try too hard to achieve something. This may seem a bit strange, but it does happen. When we want something so badly, we can often start to worry about how it will happen, when it will happen, and what you will do if it doesn't happen. I have mentioned before that we are made up of energy; a scientific fact. If we begin to try too hard and stress about the outcomes of our goals, we create negative energy and place the wrong signals out there. When we try too hard and clutter our minds with worry about something, we effectively create an energy block, which is not good. We always have to do what we can to try to achieve our goals, but excessive worry will have a negative effect and block our success. We see this a lot with people looking for relationships. They try too hard and either find nobody or the wrong person. Set goals and make plans, but then let go of stressing over outcomes, and things will begin to flow. This is called the art of surrender.

Never let pride stand in the way of happiness. Pride is fine if used in the right way, but it can also be very dysfunctional. Pride can stop us from saying sorry and making the right judgements in relationships and work. But most of all, it can stop us from asking for help. This last one can have tragic consequences. Pride will make you feel superior by not asking for help or saying sorry. However, it will really hurt and isolate you. Pride can con you into believing it is helping you, when, in fact, it is hurting you. Don't be afraid of it, but be aware, especially if you need help.

Each one us is unique. There has never been or ever will be another you. We all have our own gifts that make us special and our own ways of doing things. The problem is that we often try to compare ourselves with others and allow the judgements of others to make us feel inferior. We are not meant to be the same or do the same things as everyone else; it is impossible. Enjoy being who you were born to be, and tell yourself every day that you are proud to be you. Accept yourself lovingly and unconditionally, and see the positive changes that will take place.

Love means only good things, and love is real. This often gets confused when people talk about relationships and the problems associated with them. Real love is not difficult, judgmental, critical, too proud, or controlling. Love is about caring, giving, sharing, honesty, communication, support, and encouragement, even when times are difficult. Love has the ability to heal and bring unity. Real love does not have to be rushed; it will happen at exactly the right time. Real love must begin by finding the love within yourself. It is difficult to have a loving relationship if you do not have love and respect for yourself.

It is important that society starts placing the focus back on people. There is too much focus on money, greed, status, and power, and this is reflected in our current lifestyle. Many people lack interpersonal skills. People have become disposable and second place, which I find unacceptable. We need to learn from the past, and stop repeating the same mistakes. This change begins with all of us, and if we start with one person at a time, we will make a difference. This is about education and raising awareness in our community because we all deserve to have quality of life, not just those who make the rules.

Some necessary steps to being successful: appreciate what we have, work hard toward what we want, dream about what we would like, and learn from past mistakes. Following these steps will reduce limitations, both self-imposed and societal limitations. This may seem too simple, but it is something many of us don't do. We often fail to appreciate the wonderful people and things in life, we cease making an effort when things get too hard, we allow the past to damage our thoughts and beliefs, we focus on what is not happening, and we are too scared to dream in case of disappointment. I begin each day with giving thanks for my life, everybody in it, and everything that I have because showing gratitude encourages more positives. Every successful and happy person has had to struggle at some stage, but struggle does not mean we still can't appreciate what we have. We can even be grateful for the struggle.

Happy relationships involve having clear boundaries in place and sticking to them. If we don't, we are saying to people, "Do whatever you want, and I will put up with it." When I talk of relationships, I mean both personal and professional relationships. Boundaries really say what you think about yourself. I know this very well because for most of my life, I had no boundaries, and I attracted people who were only too happy to use and abuse me. Having boundaries does not make you cold, but it does state who you are and how you expect to be treated.

Guilt and shame are two common forms of self-sabotage. They are very destructive. Many of us suffer guilt needlessly because of society's standards and expectations. We can feel guilty because of not being able to fix other people's problems. We can feel guilty when we place our needs first. We can feel guilty because we don't live up to the standards set by our parents. We can even feel guilty when we have success or happiness.

Many of the things we feel guilty about are simply not worth our attention. Human beings are not perfect. However, many of us believe we should be. Guilt and shame eat away at us from the inside out and, in my opinion, contribute to poor physical health. Stop and really think about guilt and shame and the role they play in your life.

Don't be afraid of loving because you may get hurt.

Don't be afraid of feeling because you may cry.

Don't be afraid to dream because you may be disappointed.

Don't be afraid to live because you may die.

Just imagine for a moment if you stopped living your life by fear. Fear of being alone, fear of being ridiculed, fear of being hurt, fear of not being good enough, fear of being human, and fear of just being. I am asking you to start living life as it was meant to be lived—with passion, courage, and excitement. If you believe you can't do this, you need to seek some help.

There are many people who are totally consumed by fear and, therefore, let life pass them by. I used to let myself be controlled by fear. Now I control my fear. Life is what we make it.

Being vulnerable scares a lot of people. We don't want others to see us when we feel weak, helpless, or down. This is very understandable. The thing about vulnerability is that we are all vulnerable at some stage; I most certainly have been on many occasions. Vulnerability is actually not a weakness or any deficiency in our character. It is a feeling and a part of life. It is the ego telling us we are not worthy unless we are on top, winning and appearing strong all of the time. It is probably this message that makes us more vulnerable.

Over the years I have allowed others to see this side of me, which means that I am human. I believe this has highlighted my strengths and how far I have come. My work involves helping people who feel vulnerable, and I wouldn't be any help to them if I had not been there myself. You are not weak, but you are human. There are times we all need help, and there are times we all need to help.

If we care for ourselves and each other, we are on the way to a great life. It sounds easy, but this is not happening with a lot of people. They don't know how to really care for themselves or about themselves in an emotional and mental sense. Many people believe they are not worthy of being cared for. This can be a subconscious belief, but it is very destructive. If you can't care for yourself, it will be difficult to care for another.

One sign that people do not care for themselves can be the people they surround themselves with in relationships. People who manipulate, control, and bully them, and people who are very shallow. Other people may isolate themselves due to a lack of care, never daring to enter into a meaningful relationship. Care may sound basic and obvious, but it is not as common as it could be. It costs nothing to care, it takes no effort, and it is rewarding for everyone involved. If we all start caring, we will be happy, and the world will be a better place.

Everybody has ideas—some big, some small, and some may seem like a fantasy. The thing that successful people do is to follow through with their ideas. So many people come up with ideas that are really good but anticipate they can't work. It is too hard, not worth the risk, and a variety of other excuses deter them. I am certainly guilty of this, and it is only now that I have decided to follow through with an idea I had four years ago.

Everything starts with an idea, and it may seem hard to turn them into reality. The main thing is that we try; it doesn't matter what the idea is as long as we try. Many successful and famous people had their ideas rejected and ridiculed initially, but they went on regardless and made them happen. I know it works because I have already turned many ideas into realities. I had to ignore my fears. Idea + action = success.

Some thoughts on thoughts.

We think thousands of thoughts every single day. Thoughts are influenced by our beliefs and experiences. Every thought is a thought only in that moment. Whether a thought is true or false is irrelevant, but it will still affect us. Thoughts really do affect our reality. Thoughts have power; negative attracts negative, and positive attracts positive. When we get used to thinking certain thoughts over a significant amount of time, they are likely to continue unless we intervene. We all have a choice in every moment to change our thoughts to what we want, regardless of what is actually happening, but this can take some practice.

Thoughts need to be evaluated if they are not serving you well. What we thought and believed years ago is not our reality now and may be of no use to us today. Thoughts happen in the here and now, so we need to be living in the here and now. I hope this provokes some new thoughts in you.

I recently spoke on radio about Mental Health Awareness week. It is a reminder that there are many people and families suffering in silence, not knowing what to do or not receiving the help they require. Mental health has two aspects. There are those who suffer from a mental illness, biologically based, and those who suffer with everyday issues, emotionally based. We are all affected by emotionally based issues. The important thing is that we make time for people, and let them know we are here for them if they need us.

There is still a long way to go to educate people about mental health in general. We are all affected by mental health because we all have emotions, and we all have problems. It does not have to be that we suffer from a major mental illness. Take time out to talk with anyone you are aware of who is going through any crisis or even simply feeling down. If they don't want to talk, at least they know you care.

We are all living in an age where it is more important than ever for us to love ourselves and each other, whether it is someone we know or a complete stranger. Love is the opposite of fear, and there is much fear being spread in the community at the present time. I see many who are scared by world events and even by their personal circumstances.

The only way to stop fear is with love. Life is far too short to waste time being too scared to live. If anything, the older I get the more I long to live and experience life to the full. There have always been tragedies and disasters in the world; we are seeing some devastating things at the moment. I send love to and pray for the people affected. But if we become too scared to live, we are doing them and ourselves an injustice. Love combats fear more than anything else. I know this only too well. Live life for yourself. Live life in the present moment, and live life to spread love.

Communication is an extremely important part of life, but something that is not always used correctly. The art of communication is more than just talking and hearing. It is about getting our messages across with meaning and also really listening, not just hearing, to what is being said. Communication can be a major cause of failed relationships as well as potentially destroy careers. One of the reasons communication fails is because people are often only interested with getting their own points across. Therefore, they don't really listen to the other person.

Another problem is that we can often assume we get the meaning when we really don't. This can be due to having a vested interest in the outcome. In other words, we may hear what we want to hear. Communication is also not just about what is being said but what is not being said. Communication may require us to respond rather than react so we do get the true meaning of the message. It is a vital part of human existence.

Honesty is a very important quality to have. We often find it hard to be honest in all situations, but it is still the best option. One of the excuses we use is to say we can't be honest because it may hurt or offend someone. If it is something really important and your needs are on the line, it may be necessary to hurt someone else's feelings. Otherwise, you may be hurting yourself. Short-term pain and chaos can sometimes be necessary for long-term happiness and growth. It is not about deliberately hurting someone to be nasty. It is about doing what is best for your own self-care. If it is something unimportant, you have the option of saying nothing at all.

We also must remember to be honest with ourselves and not hide away from the truth in blissful ignorance. Honesty is a part of our true nature, and if we are not honest, we are interfering with our own happiness and that of others. Honesty is a trademark of high self-esteem. No excuses needed.

Why be ordinary when you can be extraordinary? Why place limits on who you can be and what you can achieve? There is far more to life than what we can understand with our senses. Our senses can only pick up a percentage of how life works. We often buy into the illusions of what we see, what we are told, and what we learn from society.

One of the best things I have come to learn is that we create what we are, not what we want. This means we will create anything that matches how we feel about ourselves and life, be it good or bad. If you believe you are unworthy, unloved, not good enough, or not respected or trusted, that is precisely what you will keep attracting into your life. If you believe you are worthy, deserving, loved, or abundant, then that is what you will attract. This needs to be more than just said; it needs to be felt. We need to understand just how powerful we are and what power our thoughts and beliefs have. I will no longer place limits on what I can achieve, and I will never think poorly of myself again because I deserve the best, as you all do. See beyond the surface, and push yourself to the limits to create happiness.

As a younger man, I wanted to be liked by everyone. If someone didn't like me, I took it very personally, sometimes worrying about it for days. If someone said hurtful comments to me, I automatically believed it without question. If I failed at something, I would never try it again, and it seriously degraded my confidence. There were times that I just wanted to be invisible and make the world go away. Clearly, I didn't like myself very much—despite what I may have shown to others. This was a lonely sort of existence in my inner world of dysfunctional and destructive thoughts. This is common for many.

My awakening came when I realised the most important person who needed to like me was me. Then I realised that hurtful comments were a reflection of the people saying them, not me. The only failure in life was the failure not to try, and the grand finale thought was that I was being my own worst enemy and that nobody else was responsible for my feelings. Today, I love being me, and my life is more wonderful than I ever could have imagined. Be true to yourself by being yourself, loving yourself, and respecting your own unique nature.

Rejection can be one of the hardest experiences to deal with. Having a partner leave you or wanting to be with somebody who doesn't want to be with you are both painful experiences. The situation can be heightened if you do not have high self-esteem or self-worth. Throughout all my learning in life, I have realised everything, including rejection, comes down to a state of mind; how we perceive everything. I have experienced this on more than one occasion.

With rejection, it is important to acknowledge and express your feelings, and talk with somebody who you trust. It is good to talk with a counsellor and analyse what has actually happened in the relationship. Another important aspect is to focus on yourself and not the other person. Be kind and patient with yourself. Treat yourself to things you enjoy. Spend some quality time with yourself, family, and friends. Do not take it as a criticism of the person you are; do not reject yourself. No matter how much you may love someone, it is no good being with him or her if you are not loved in the same way. Take time to work through this process, and know you only deserve the best.

It is important to start your day well and end your day well. Then everything in between will fall into place. My day always begins with meditation, giving gratitude for all I have, saying affirmations, and then having breakfast. Before I go to sleep, I once again meditate, do affirmations, and give gratitude. When I am in bed, I focus on the good feelings that are associated with all I want to achieve. Some mornings I walk and sometimes I do it in the evening; exercise is very important.

Too many times people start their day with a negative outlook and set themselves up for a negative day. It is the same when we go to bed with negative thoughts; they encourage more negativity the following day. When we wake up, we can be grateful for simply being alive and well. When we go to bed, we can be grateful for all the blessings we have and often take for granted.

We will never understand everything in this life. And the good news is that we don't have to. There are so many mysteries that nobody can explain, not even science. Personally, I do not need an explanation for everything that happens. For me, it is a feeling of just knowing that something exists or that something just works. I find life a lot easier this way, and it is also far more exciting.

If you limit yourself to pure factual evidence, you will be doing yourself a great disservice. We need to understand that life is not just about facts, figures, numbers, and statistics. Life is about living, feeling, and believing. Open your heart and your mind to the endless possibilities that are around you every day.

The most important people to be charitable to are those in your immediate vicinity, those in your community who you come into contact with daily, whether they be family, friends, colleagues, or strangers. These are the people you can influence with love and kindness and be in a position to help. It does not need to be anything major. Just doing anything at all to help somebody in need, even if it is giving a compliment, will have a positive impact for everyone. Helping those in your community will help the community grow in general. There are many deserving causes all over the world, but if you start with those in your presence, you will be laying a strong foundation for spreading charity all over the world.

We may be ridiculed for what we believe, think, or say, and that is okay. The important thing is that we always come from a place of honesty and sincerity regardless of the opinions of others. When we truly believe in what we say, do, and think, we will never be afraid of the judgements and criticisms of others. This is a sign of real maturity and freedom. We can't and won't have everybody agree with us or our opinions. That is because we are all unique individuals with varying levels of experience and wisdom. Being honest with ourselves about our beliefs and values allows us to gain self-respect and a true feeling of empowerment.

My world is everything I can imagine it to be. It is everything I want it to be and everything I put into it. My world is directly connected to how I feel, think, and believe. My world is a reflection of how I have grown from the lessons I have learnt. If I become unhappy with my world, I have the power and control to fix it. In my world, I do not have to rely on or blame anyone else because I take responsibility for my world and my happiness. I love my world.

There is no dress rehearsal for life. We need to live it right here and right now. This means we need to get over regrets and mistakes from our past. We need to stop comparing ourselves to others. We need to follow our hearts, not our minds. We need to be willing to confront pain and then let go of it. We need to become assertive to let others know we are in charge of our lives. But most of all, we need to know we are good enough and always have been. Wasting time in life is simply unacceptable, especially when we have the ability and right to do whatever we want. Nothing in life is guaranteed, but all things are possible. Time to swing into action and be the creator of your own destiny. Enjoying life means experimenting with it, so have fun and make the most of your life.

One of the greatest myths in life is that we are our bodies and minds. This is incorrect. We are our souls, which can be called the real self, higher-self, or eternal self. The reason this is who we really are is that the soul is where all our love, wisdom, goodness, and intention come from. It is eternal. When we talk of the body or mind, we are relating more to the ego. The ego is where we find fear, hate, insecurity, jealousy, doubt, anxiety, and depression. Everything that comes from the real self, which includes difficult lessons, cause us to grow, learn, and become the best person we can be. Everything that comes from the ego leads to isolation, separation, confusion, and sadness. A soul will never criticise you and tell you that you are unworthy or unlovable. However, the ego will, but not just your ego but the ego of others. We need our bodies, minds, and egos. It is important, however, we realise that we are far more than these aspects of ourselves.

Generosity is a quality I admire greatly. Generosity goes beyond being generous with money or material items. The greatest way to be generous is with your heart and time. Giving of one's personality and experience can change someone's life. I know so many generous and caring people who make me feel very blessed. I know the massive difference they have made to my life, especially because I know they are coming from the heart.

We all have something to share with others, no matter how trivial it may seem. A few caring words, half an hour of your time, and a listening ear can have an amazing effect on someone's day. Generosity is an expression of love, and it can only lead to a better future.

Despite all the theories, therapies, and medications that are around these days, the most effective form of healing is compassion. To be in the moment with someone, be there intently for them with the intention of supporting and genuinely caring about them, is the most powerful therapy of all. Treating people as people and not problems is essential. This is what I have based my business around, and I find the results speak for themselves.

Any form of therapy can't be rushed, and there is a process to follow. But the work involved is worth the time when you see results. We live in times where a quick fix is the order of the day, but a quick fix is not a lasting fix. Life experience, intention to help, and demonstrating compassion are the best tools a counsellor can have.

Anything worthwhile usually requires a struggle in some form. Having to struggle to achieve goals makes them so much more gratifying and fulfilling. Looking for the easy road will not bring us closer to our goals but will drive us further away. Struggle brings growth, power, wisdom, and achievement. We should never be afraid of struggle because it is a natural part of life. Working hard and confronting obstacles is a necessary part of life. It is through this process that we find the real joy in our achievements and successes. Be determined to achieve your dreams. And most important, be willing to do whatever it takes achieve them.

Being involved with someone in an intimate relationship does not mean you become his or her life. Being involved intimately with someone means you enhance that person's life as yours is enhanced by him or her. We must remember that when entering a relationship, we do not cease being our own person. The relationship is made up of two individuals, both with their own needs, desires, and purposes. When we truly love another, we need to ensure that our needs are met and that we are satisfied with ourselves before we can truly give fully of ourselves.

Too many people believe the other person has to be their lives. They sacrifice their own needs and desires to please him or her. This achieves nothing but resentment and unhappiness. Happy relationships begin with two happy people who truly enhance the lives of each other because their own lives are fulfilling and purposeful.

Printed in the United States
By Bookmasters